"WHAT AM I GOING TO DO WITH THIS CHILD?"

3 EASY STEPS to SUCCESSFUL PARENTING

Karen McKenzieSmith

Copyright © 2015 by Karen McKenzieSmith

ISBN: 978-0-9921428-10

Published by Speaking Presence Publishing

Printed in Canada. All rights reserved. No part of this book may be used in any way or reproduced in any manner without the express written permission of the Author.

Although the Author has made every effort to ensure that the information in this book was correct at press time, the Author does not assume liability to any party for any loss, damage, or disruption caused by errors or omissions, whether such errors or omissions result from negligence, accident, or any other cause.

Wholesale: Quantity discounts are available on bulk purchases of this book for reselling, educational resources, gifts or fundraising. For more information please contact the Author at:

karencowgirl@shaw.ca

TABLE OF CONTENTS

PROLOGUE 1

CHAPTER 1: How I Know This Will Work 5

CHAPTER 2: Discipline Works! 7

CHAPTER 3: The 3 Step Discipline Process .. 11

CHAPTER 4 **Step 1**: *Describe The Specific Behaviour You Expect* 13

CHAPTER 5 **Step 2**: *Set And Communicate Reasonable Consequences* 25

CHAPTER 6 **Step 3**: *Be Consistent* 61

CHAPTER 7: Attitude 69

CHAPTER 8: Being Assertive While Communicating 74

CHAPTER 9: Planning Your Activities 78

CHAPTER 10: Conclusion 81

IN SUMMARY 85

PROLOGUE

Do you know that not disciplining a child is an act of negligence and is really a form of hate rather than of love?

By using the 3 easy steps to discipline outlined in this booklet, you are benefiting your child.

Which of these scenarios would you rather face?

➢ Nagging throughout a morning to get your child up and going.

OR

➢ No nagging because your child knows the natural consequences if they are late.

****

➢ Screaming displays to avoid the real problem.

OR

➢ No emotional outburst because your child knows that natural consequences will occur even if they act out so they don't bother.

****

➢ Acting like a "victim" as a reaction to the child's behaviour. For example saying, "Now we're late because of you!" This teaches a child they can control the parent's mood as well as their day! Worse yet, the parent suffers more than the child and wants to avoid an incident.

OR

➢ A child that knows they can't control the family's mood or time. That child then has the opportunity to grow as they are allowed to suffer the cost of a natural consequence.

In this book, I discuss an amazing and simple *3 step discipline* process that can help you help your child to achieve good behaviour, most of the time.

Curious to know more?
Let's get started.

CHAPTER 1:

How I Know This Will Work

I am a person that writes about what I believe in. When teaching post-graduate courses, I taught this simple and effective method of discipline in a Family Studies course for parents.

What I am going to share with you in this book is tried and true. It really works! How do I know this? As both a parent and a teacher, I have succeeded in using this method of parenting. In addition I have taught this method to numerous parents that have used it with great results.

In my profession as a teacher, not once did I need to raise my voice to get children to do what they were asked to and needed to do. Not once as a parent, did I have to use force with my own children or raise my voice with them either.

As the mother of three strong-willed children, I can assure you that this technique was a breeze to carry out. Discipline was never easier, not only with my determined boys but my daughter as well.

In the chapters that follow, I will explain the 3 simple things you need to do to achieve effective and successful discipline for stress-free parenting.

Near the end of this booklet, I have one final secret to reveal that will set your whole mind at ease about using these 3 steps.

CHAPTER 2:

Discipline Works!

Properly planned and calmly administered discipline is not abusive. It can be argued that a lack of discipline is abuse, as it can hamper your child, keeping them emotionally immature and incapable of making positive decisions.

Who should bear the repercussions of a child's misbehaviour? You or the child? Is it you that should learn or the child? And is it not worthwhile for them to learn?

Write here your thoughts on each of the above questions so you have them down on paper. Also, it is important for you the parent right now to put in your own words how you know that it is not abusive for your child to experience the repercussions of their own bad behaviour or their own actions in logical and natural ways. Note that I said in natural and logical ways.

// How I feel about discipline:

One thing that children tend to do is confuse the issue by not feeling comfortable with discipline, or claiming that they are not able to behave etc. Then a parent without boundaries comes to their rescue, short-circuiting effective discipline. This is a big mistake, for it prevents the child from learning the difference between what they can't do and what is just hard to do.

Letting your child deal with reality is a good thing. It is inevitable that they will experience growing pains. A parent can oversee this to assure the pains are not ones of injury but logical and natural ones that won't result in injury. They are simply good, long-lasting lessons learned to develop sterling and superior maturity. That's a quality outcome for your child! Don't you agree?

It takes time to plan and administer discipline, but it is worth it, because it will result in children that are able to:

- ✓ be responsible for their problems;

- ✓ admit when they are wrong;

- ✓ pick themselves up when they fail and forgive;

- ✓ change their mind, behaviour or direction once they understand the consequences;

- ✓ conquer troubles; and

- ✓ have the courage to fight their battles or let some go.

So, now that we have introduced the reasons why it works, and is important to healthy child development, let's take a look at the overall process.

CHAPTER 3:

The 3 Step Discipline Process

#1. Describe the Specific Behaviour You Expect

#2. Set and Communicate Reasonable Consequences

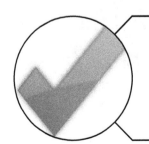

#3. Apply Consistently

The previous table shows the simple 3 Step Discipline process that we outline in this booklet.

We will outline the steps in detail, and give lots of examples, so that by the end of the booklet you will be very familiar with the method.

CHAPTER 4

Step 1: *Describe The Specific Behaviour You Expect*

The first step is one that parents often forget to implement. I discovered as I conducted parenting courses on discipline that many parents did not think of this step, or think that they needed to describe the specific behaviour they expect from their children. By neglecting this key step they were missing a very important piece to parental discipline that makes it work much more smoothly.

You hear parents time and time again say something like this: "Now you behave!"

What is that supposed to mean? Behave how? Does a young child know exactly how they are supposed to behave in all situations? Of course not! That is why parents, in order to be successful, need to include this all-important step. Therefore, the first step in successful discipline is to:

Describe the Specific Behaviours Wanted

When we ask children to behave, do they know how? Do they know what that means in each and every situation? Especially if they are to behave in this particular way for the very first time. Take, for example, their first time at a swimming pool, theatre or movie, symphony or hockey game. They may not know what is wanted.

If expected behaviour is explained, which in a way, is the same as establishing boundaries, then you are not only disciplining them but helping them develop a conscience. In so doing they grow up more responsible and mature.

They also gain many other attributes:

- ➤ They determine a clear sense of who they are.
- ➤ They develop an understanding of what they are responsible for.

➢ They practice a working ability to make choices,
➢ They also learn what occurs when they make good or bad choices, (that things will go well or they will not). There are natural and logical consequences of their choices. This concept is most important for them to learn in childhood, and as early in life as possible.

All of the above contribute to the development of a mature and well-rounded adult.

It is important to know the main roles we have as parents. We are basically meant to be our children's guardians, managers, and main source to learn by.

➢ **Guardians**: provide the basic necessities of life for a child. This primarily means, shelter, protection and provision. We utilize our experiences with wisdom to provide that right amount of balance between freedom and limits to their environment. This makes for a safe, yet fun-filled learning field for them to explore.

➢ **Managers**: besides managing their safety, we make sure that the responsibilities, expectations and requirements made of them are achieved. We parents manage and teach them how to deal with life's demands as well as helping them set goals to encourage them and help them to grow into productive adults.

We constructively direct our children in finding the many ways to accomplish goals, and they learn of course, whether by successes or through mistakes made along the way. For we then help them learn how to continue after such inevitable failures and disappointments.

➢ **Sources**: Parents as sources are the number one resource our children have and can come to for the basic necessities of life and all the good things too.

Overall, parents teach and interject with consequences which are appropriate boundaries to guard our children from the many dangers they can face at any given time.

I do not think that many parents realize when taking their children to events they have never been to before; that their children likely have no clue what to do when asked to "behave yourself." Therefore the first step is to clarify what behaviour is expected from them in any given situation.

After doing so you immediately follow up with what will happen if they do not behave the way they are expected to. As well as what can happen if they behave the way you expect them to. This is what STEP 2 is all about. I will discuss this in the next chapter.

EXAMPLE:
Pulling into a grocery store parking lot.

Once parked, take the time in the car to describe to your children how you expect them to behave when they go in to the store, if you have not done so already. In fact you can even remind them if they need a reminder. **i.e.:** "Sit quietly in the shopping cart without reaching for or grabbing items off the shelves." You also need to let them know that you expect that there will be no complaining or arguing or screaming, crying, yelling, or acting up of any kind.

If they are older, explain that they are to stay with you and maybe push the grocery cart. This will keep them busy but more importantly let them be and feel useful. Children like to know they can contribute to the adult world of their parents.

APPLY TO YOUR SITUATION

Add a description in your own words here, on what **STEP 1** is all about:

_____
_____
_____
_____

_____

_____

_____

_____

_____

_____

_____

_____

EXAMPLE

Here is one of my own examples I recall. It was a visit to the Calgary Zoo. Since my boys were older and of an adventuresome age, (about 5 & 8), they were to stay in our sight and not run off on their own. I also explained the dangers involved if they did run off to explore on their own, which was definitely something my boys would do. I did not fill them with fear as I explained this part, but I did stress the need to stick close together.

I went on to describe what to do if we did get separated. I made sure they remembered what entrance to meet at and where they should go to if we got separated. I directed them if possible, to find a security guard or staff member for help.

How is that for STEP 1? Isn't it nice and simple? Now all you have to do is to implement it consistently. (That is a bit harder, but I know you can do it!)

APPLY TO YOUR SITUATION

Take time now to describe other behaviours you expect to see from your child/ren for further different scenarios.

> Visiting an amusement park:

_____
_____
_____
_____
_____
_____
_____
_____
_____
_____
_____

➢ Visiting Grandma or other relatives:

➢ Visiting the doctor or dentist:

➢ Shopping in the mall:

> List other situations that you want to plan for, and the behaviours you expect here, and on the next page:

KAREN MCKENZIESMITH

CHAPTER 5

Step 2: *Set And Communicate Reasonable Consequences*

This step is one that takes a bit more thinking but again it is easily do-able. After explaining how your child/ren should behave in the varied, individual environments, it is equally important that you set consequences for wrong behaviour. You need to let them know what happens if they choose not to behave as asked.

EXAMPLE If your child/ren ignore requests to clean up their room (having had what "clean" means spelled out in clear terms) your response is firm but not said in an angry tone.

Simply say: "I will only ask once (or maybe you choose to say twice), for you to clean up your room. You have 30 minutes to clean it up. Then you can go out to play. If you don't, you will miss out being able to… i.e.: Go play with your friends sooner, if at all, depending on how long you take to clean up."

Especially if they are not yet used to the type of discipline that sets consequences and follows through, they may yell and scream and carry-on. Your response is unfaltering. In an even tone showing that you are not bothered, you the parent simply state calmly, "Until you can talk respectfully in a proper manner to me, your liberties will be on hold."

This is what I call a "teachable moment." It can be used to teach a child that they will not be heard and respected when they speak to others in a disrespectful manner.

Reassure them that once they speak civilly to you, they will be listened to. It may not mean they will get what they want but they will at least be listened to respectfully.

THE IMPORTANCE OF PLANNING AHEAD

Part A: Plan Consequences Ahead

A problem I found parents in my sessions expressed was that they just could not come up with a consequence fast enough to deal with the different situations and variety of misbehaviours they would possibly contend with. This can be the step that is the most difficult for parents to carry out.

It is hard to come up with logical consequences when the child or children are misbehaving around you. When you do not come up with something, they may not take you seriously. It can make the whole process of the discipline potentially unsuccessful.

I want to stop here and strongly suggest that you plan what consequences you will use ahead of time. It is too difficult to try to come up with various consequences on the spot. Hence taking time to make lists can help.

It is a great idea to pause now, when you have the time. Now you can think clearly to build your personal arsenal. Creating a list here of possible consequences will make it much easier for you to come up with a suitable and effective one on the spur of the moment.

Therefore, I strongly advise parent(s) to list consequences ahead of time to fall back on as a valuable resource.

It is a good idea to have made this list ahead to utilize so you don't run into the same problems other parents have experienced.

Basically, if you drop the ball at this stage of discipline you undermine your authority as a parent in front of your child or children.

It is important that consequences be **logical** consequences. Choose consequences that suit or fit the crime, and consequences that are associated with things the child values. We parents need to file in our memory banks a few logical consequences.

Now let's get busy! List some consequences you as parents can live with. It would be great if the two of you, (husband and wife), could work together on these lists so that both of you can be on the same page with your disciplining. The more support you as husband and wife in this job called parenting can give each other the better off each of you will be. It will also show the children that they can't play each parent off of the other. This is regardless of whether you are still together or separate and on your own, it is still important to discipline together, using the same method if at all possible. If not, it is still important for at least one parent to be consistent with the usage of these three important steps.

Here are a couple of examples to get you started with your list of consequences:

EXAMPLE:
A very common time when discipline is needed is car trips. I would carry a book or magazine to read or some knitting. So while driving I could pull over for however long it took after giving them a warning for the kids

to settle down. If they did not obey, I did not have to suffer the wait, as I had something good on hand to do until they settled down to allow me to continue on, safely, driving.

EXAMPLE:
When they wouldn't pick their toys up and put them away when asked, I would rake the toys up and put them in a garbage bag to give away to their friends when they came over to play.

I would tell them what would happen if they didn't clean up and what would happen if they did. I would set the stove timer so as to make it fun for them to race against the clock while picking up their toys.

Actually, they didn't do it the first time. No sirree, they did not lift a finger. So I had to follow through on my consequence that I laid out when I asked them to pick up their toys.

That is the KEY point right there! You have to do what you said you would. That is why I impress upon you that it is necessary to come up with a list of consequences that you are willing to follow through on.

I did what I said I would. I gathered up all the toys myself and put them in a garbage bag. Then I couldn't wait for one of their friends to come over so that I could pull that bag out and let them pick a toy to take home.

Of course my boys had a fit! One thing they said that was just perfect, was, "You can't give that toy away. It is my favourite toy!"

My reply back in a very CALM and NEUTRAL VOICE, was "Well it could not have been that important to you if you did not want to take care of it and pick it up when I asked you to."

The nice thing about it that you will be relieved to know; is the happy ending that I will leave to share, at the end of this booklet, as the best for last.

It is important to follow through with positive reinforcement from time to time as well. For example, after asking them to behave in a grocery store, when they do so, buy them a treat or stop for ice cream cones on the way home, etc. By so doing, you are putting the focus on the benefits of good behaviour.

Write your list of potential consequences:

Misbehaviour:_____

Consequences:_____
_____
_____
_____
_____
_____
_____

Misbehaviour:_____

Consequences_____
_____
_____
_____
_____

WHAT AM I GOING TO DO WITH THIS CHILD?

_____

_____

Misbehaviour:_____

Consequences:_____

_____

_____

_____

_____

_____

Misbehaviour:_____

Consequences:_____

_____

_____

_____

_____

_____

Misbehaviour:_____

Consequences:_____

_____

_____

_____
_____
_____
_____

Misbehaviour:_____

Consequences:_____
_____
_____
_____
_____
_____

Misbehaviour:_____

Consequences:_____
_____
_____
_____
_____
_____

Please Note:

If you don't set up consequences for your dear children, LIFE WILL!

However, never fear, I have a solution to this problem in order for you to be successful. In fact I have a few solutions to assure success in carrying out Step 2.

There are times when consequences can be **natural** ones too. For example, one obvious one is: If they go outside on a cold winter day without a coat; they will certainly be very cold. Hence they will experience a natural consequence of such an action.

When these natural consequences occur it is important as a parent to avoid saying things like: "I told you so!...or… "I warned you!" I don't just say this because it isn't nice. And because it is not a competition between parent and a child, whereby you're keeping score. I say this for this important reason: It is a way to give your children the freedom to change their minds. In other words, if they naturally find themselves cold and come back in to get a coat.

It is wiser for the parent to say something like: "Good, I'm glad you changed your mind." or "Oh good, I am glad you made a better choice." This allows you to take opportunities such as this to teach through encouragement, which is a very effective way to teach children. It is a chance for you the parent to teach your child that they can have the freedom to change their minds and make better choices.

If we as parents want to show them up we are only hindering our own process of parenting by doing so. If we hold the criticism back and avoid saying, "I told you so!" then we are subliminally teaching them that they can change their mind and mind-set in the long run, for the better. Children are more likely to change their minds and do the right thing if they don't decide that they must remain stubborn and dig their heels because they hear their parent's jabs. Jabs like, "I told you so!" or "When are you ever going to learn?"

I hope you see the importance of not getting pitted against your kids. By watching and curtailing negative comments you will prevent pitting yourself against your kids. Instead you can show them they can make good choices for themselves, even if it was not their first choice.

Now you are probably thinking: How am I going to remember to carry this list around to refer to? Well, I find if one gets to write down ideas, they are more than likely to recall those ideas.

Add a description below, in your own words, on what STEP 2 is all about:

_____
_____
_____
_____
_____
_____
_____
_____
_____
_____

Part B: Have your Child/ren Come up with Their Own Consequences

As we have seen, in Step 2 a parent needs to have a consequence to carry out if the child misbehaves.

Besides making a list ahead, I have a few solutions that can help you come up with good consequences. This is a sure-fire solution for you if you draw a blank when trying on the spot to come up with a good consequence for their misbehaviour.

Here is the way out if you can't come up with a solution of your own on the spot. Have your child come up with their own. Ask them what they think the consequence should be for their wrong actions.

This does two things:

1) When the child suggests a consequence of their own for themselves; they tend to come up with a stiffer one all on their own than you the parent would implement.

2) Also, it can trigger you to quickly think of something good that can apply, as you discuss it together.

Now here is the best part about asking the child to decide a consequence for themselves. As I said, they tend to come up with something more severe than required for that particular incident. So you as the parent can come out of it smelling like a rose. Since their idea usually is more severe and you the parent waters it down, you end up looking really good. That is a life saver! Taking the severe suggestion they gave you and lessening its severity makes your child feel that you have given them some slack, and that you have been merciful unto them. Yet you are still disciplining them. Now that has to be a good outcome all round, wouldn't you say? If they catch on and water their OWN consequence down themselves, you can then revise it a bit, so as not to get caught if and when the older child/teen may try it. That way the consequence remains reasonable. Either way, letting them voice what they think may be a relevant consequence is still helpful for them as well as you the parent. It can still be utilized as a guide one way or another.

Before I come to a close on STEP 2, I have a few important pointers I hope you will keep in mind while carrying out justified consequences:

A) Use Natural Consequences

I believe it is important to leave the word "punishment" out of conversations over consequences. Number one; they are not the same thing. Two, the child grows up learning that there are consequences for their actions. They learn that there is an opposite and equal reaction to their actions. That they have to be held accountable for what they choose to do. This in turn develops conscience, responsibility and maturity.

Our children really need boundaries. To them this can at first appear as confusing, and of course their reaction can be to them the end of the world and they can potentially complain like it is. However as a parent, just keep telling yourself that it is necessary for them to grow to maturity and for their survival. Believe it or not their protests are a normal part of growing up. They need to do this in order to become responsible adults, and to be able to be self-sufficient and fend for themselves. It helps them differentiate good choices from bad/evil choices.

A clue to picking out the right consequence is to pick one that is going to cost them something they value. Children's behaviour of today rarely costs them anything. It seems to have no consequences and does not become a problem for them, but it should. If they don't suffer consequences for their bad behaviour, they will never learn from it nor establish boundaries for themselves. As parents we are doing them a disservice by not holding them accountable for their actions.

Naturally there is an opposite and equal reaction for every action. By letting your children experience the reaping of what they sow they see in living colour their irresponsibility and reap the natural consequences. Unfortunately, parents find it hard to let their child go through natural consequences. Parents may even look like they don't care if they let their children deal with their natural consequences. Sure the reality-based consequences they reap may seem painful for your child and painful for you to watch, but I can assure you the success in the long run, far outweighs the immediate pain.

A parent must avoid psychological consequences and allow the child to bear the reality of the natural and or logical consequences that occur when their child is held accountable.

B) **Work Together** When coming up with a list of possible consequences it is ideal for both parents to work together.

This applies equally whether you are still married or not. It is best for both of you to be on the same page when it comes to carrying out disciplinarian action. It prevents the child or children from playing you against each other. Obviously it is a much better way to deal with discipline if both parents agree.

C) **Avoid Making Yourself Suffer** Most important of all, is to make consequences that do not make you the parent, or other family members suffer in any way if possible.

For example, in the case of going shopping, if they do misbehave and you lay down the consequence that you will go home if they misbehave, then it should be fine by you to go home. After all, technically, you can go shop anytime. So it is not as much of a big deal if you do have to drop everything and go home. However, if you say the same thing when you are all going on a holiday or outing, having to go home is punishing you and the rest of the family. This is simply an inappropriate consequence to uphold, and not one you would want to use nor follow through on.

That is why thinking up appropriate consequences is so important. Even saying we are going home if you misbehave while shopping may or may not be the best consequence depending on the situation at the time. Therefore you would want to have another consequence.

EXAMPLE:

Our family was going on an outing and the one of the kids was acting up in the back of the Suburban. Their father yelled back at them to be quiet or he would turn us around and go home. After saying this a few times it got to the point that he was going to have to follow through or look like a parent that could be walked all over, teaching the kids that they need not take his threats seriously.

The disaster about this scenario was that the rest of us were behaving just fine! Especially me the mom in the front passenger seat!

I felt I was between a rock and a hard place because I did not want to interject and counter their dad's way of handling it. I did not want the children to see I was not in favour of their father's decision. They did not need to see we were not on the same page when it came to discipline. I was also looking forward to the outing and sure did not want to miss out on it by turning around and going home! So I leaned over and quietly said to him that I was behaving and looking forward to the outing. Therefore could we come up with a consequence that did not mean turning around and going back home?

EXAMPLE:

Here is how I handled the situation when on my own with the kids while driving. Remember I gave this as an example earlier on. I am referring to it again to shed light on another important factor. I would tell them that they needed to settle down or I would have to pull over and wait until they did, so that it would be safe to drive. It is important and useful to both you the parent and the child to state WHY you need to stop the vehicle. Then they are assured that you are not just being a dictator on a power trip. It teaches them that you are watching out for them and their best interests.

After giving them 2 chances to settle down in which case they did not, I would pull over like I said I would. I remember one time I did this, that it was actually kind of funny how it all happened. The first few minutes was taken up with them realizing I actually had pulled over. The next few minutes were used up with them blaming each other. The next few minutes between them, were used by them to get each other to be quiet. LOL!

Now I just want to take time here to clarify, that the consequence I used did not punish me as well. What I would do back then, was carry a good book to read. Therefore, at any time when I had to do something like exit, I would pull out my book and catch up on my reading. So however long they were going to take to settle down so I could pull back on to the road and continue on; it didn't matter because I was enjoying my book! Yeah!

So the point I want to stress is: find a way to carry out the consequence without it being a hindrance on you. If it is a hindrance to you, it is not a logical and natural consequence for them and them alone, as it should be.

The consequence must fit the crime, so to speak. It also must not inconvenience you the parent either. For you are not the one triggering the natural and or logical consequences. Therefore do not cause yourself to suffer along with them.

So you not only state clearly the behaviour desired and WHY, as is necessary in STEP 1. It is important to follow through and describe STEP 2, the consequence, as well. The child, and you the parent need to know what consequences will be followed through on when and if they cross over the boundaries you have plainly laid out for them. This keeps it all clear, above board and has everyone on the same page and knowing what is going on.

Our children need to learn how to grow with boundaries. We as parents are their primary influencers in this department. The three main ways we can be this for them are by: teaching, modeling and helping them to internalize.

Teaching: We teach our children so many things. Some of those things can be inconsequential or can be paramount for their wellbeing. One of those is their ability to hear clearly and to say "No" in okay ways. This allows them to change their mind. It gives them the chance to back out.

Of course it is understandable that teachings will adapt to differences in ages from birth to eighteen years of age. Therefore, I'm including here a description of the differences a parent can generally expect from their child/ren at these varying age levels.

It is a rough guideline that shows the basic kind of variance in understanding, and thus appropriate discipline at various age ranges. By variance, I'm referring to the cognitive age of a child at the different stages in their life and how they perceive discipline and the dynamics of the learning they go through chronologically at the different age levels. In reality, it stands to reason that a child in the first years of their life is going to receive discipline and acknowledge it entirely differently than when the same child deals with it and understands all the dynamics of it as a teenager.

I've broken down a child's life span into the standard five age stages:

<u>Birth to twelve months -</u> First and foremost, infants are bonding with their parents. This

establishes their sense of security and trust in us as their mother or father. As little ones they haven't enough love and data collected within their little minds to handle a lot of frustration in the beginning. Plus boundaries are few and less is required in their very first year of growing up but it is still important to implement in order to get that all significant early start. It is all about us as parents building a trust by maintaining those necessities of life filled with nurturing through love and comfort and providing for all that babies require.

<u>One to three years of age—</u> During this stage, parents teach our children to respond correctly to the word "NO." Children also learn the consequences of their disobedience to that word, for example, when there are dangers, such as touching the hot stove anyway when told of the dangers and not to. It doesn't necessarily mean they get the logic behind it all at this age or younger. It more than likely makes sense to them knowing that good things happen to them when they obey and bad consequences happen when they don't obey.

<u>Three to five years old—</u>   At this age, children begin to understand the reasons for being responsible. They can also understand what consequences are all about. This can be an enjoyable age for us as parents to go through, for it is when they themselves can discuss these things with us. This age is where we can teach them how to disagree in good ways without fighting, by being respectful, treating their friends nicely, respecting authority and learning all about chores and fulfilling them. Consequences for this age come mostly in the form of loss of use of game-boys, TV, toys or fun events and activities. These boundary-type consequences are very effective at this age, which means you the parent have more things like their toys and TV to hold over them as consequences.

<u>Six to eleven years—</u> The consequential field broadens the older a child gets. Now boundaries involve school, clubs, friends, entertainment, activities of sorts and so forth. Boundaries with budgeting their money as well as time become paramount. What they

value at this age revolves around limits with friends, time on their own, chores and privileges.

<u>Twelve to eighteen years—</u>   The teen years are the last before adulthood. As teens establish their identities, the parent begins to allow distance by becoming a "parent of influence" rather than one in a controlling place. Here is where we can subtly guide our teens with greater issues like morals, consciences, goals and relationships. This is where they show their growth in maturity. The more they indicate their maturity in being responsible, the more freedom is given by the parent(s).

EXAMPLE:

An issue with my own son revolved around curfew. He was being a real block-head about demanding his curfew be extended. I stated that I was not going to listen to any of his "talk with attitude" and complaining.

"Bottom-line," I told him, "if you whine like that you will get nowhere but a definite NO. Ask me in a polite manner and I will make a decision."

He had to first be willing to talk in a civilized manner that was not like a Bart Simpson type character. Then I was willing to hear him out.

After a few more attempts that fell on my deaf ears, he changed his tone. So I wholeheartedly said "You bet, let's sit down and talk. Would you like a juice or pop?" (I wanted to reward his change of character with the pop and show him the respect he should get for having the right approach and change of attitude.) He actually asked for a half-hour extension on the curfew. So I said "Okay, why not? You have shown that you are responsible in many ways like getting home on time when asked. So let's give it a try."

Little did he know that I had been going to give him an hour extension. He showed he was able to handle coming home on time with the half-hour extension he asked for. Given that, I soon after told him I was very pleased with how he was handling it, and I gave him an additional half-hour.

Out of that interchange around the curfew, my son was able to learn a lot about growing up and how to be heard and get what he wanted. A good start to his teenage years, I would have to say.

Modeling: How we the parent handle our boundaries, and our natural and logical consequences gives the child food for thought to better learn by.

Internalizing: We can help children experience situations and approaches that help them along in life. It is not just "the knowing" a child needs to learn, but allowing them to experience the reality of the knowledge by living through consequences. That type of knowledge is a far better asset to have. Another reality that is valuable to learn, for both parent and child, is to help and not rescue. There is a big difference. It is hard for a parent not to step in and keep their child from suffering the natural and logical consequences of their actions. If you keep in mind that you do not do your child any favours by sparing them the consequences, you will raise a capable and responsible child. You will have helped them greatly by not rescuing them, thus reducing their chances of being irresponsible instead.

Internalizing for a child is fundamental to establishing the ability to love and build a conscience. This is where right and wrong and self-control grow. Along with this, the parent(s) might hear their child or children speak harshly to themselves when they misbehave. You may even hear them say they "hate you." No worries, for this is a good thing, believe it or not! It means they have begun to mature and become aware of their actions and the results of those actions.

I think youngsters of today are confused as to what their limits are and are really screaming out for parents to show them their boundaries, hence pushing the envelope.

Parents, out of guilt or fear of conflict, do their teens no good by not providing the necessary boundaries. Hence teens act out even more to provoke limits or even worse; push the envelope if they feel they have a sense of entitlement.

There has to be a happy medium in a child having power. The right amount promotes a realistic sense of control within themselves which is a good thing. On the other hand too much power given them, produces a lack of respect for others, which I am sure you discern is not good.

Make note that children do not realize they are not the center of the universe and that they are not immortal in regards to their lives and time. They think they have insurmountable energy to handle it all! Surprise, surprise, this only results in problems with overextending themselves.

You the parent, however, can gently guide them and encourage them in discovering that they are not immortal. This can be achieved by letting your child trap themselves in their own vicious circle of commitments. They will soon experience the natural consequences of their dilemma. By all means, let them feel the consequences, while still being supportive emotionally, for that will be the best way they can learn to manage their time better.

EXAMPLE:

Parent: *You can't go to the movies until you have done your chores.*

Child: *I hate your rules! It's just not fair!*

P: *I know it can be frustrating when you forgot about chores and now have no time to do both.*

 PLEASE NOTE:

It is important to not shame and or blame the child or even defend yourself as a parent. Yet it is okay to understand and empathize as you stand firm in a neutral manner regarding the chores.

We sometimes wonder why our children do some of the things they do. Well this is why: in their learning process, they think they are invincible and will not experience the outcome of their actions. We all did it.

Sometimes kids may lie, contrive, manipulate, distort and rationalize. Whatever to avoid accountability. As I have already said, you do not do them a service if you help them avoid consequences. You need to help them learn that they are not infallible. That they can learn from the natural and logical consequences of their failures and grow from them. To learn they are not the controller of others but that they can learn with your help that the only one they can control is themselves.

Beware also of making your child or children, your BFF, your friend. Some parents may think it is cool to have their son or daughter as a best friend. A confidant to share their problems with. What really happens, is you turn them into a parent for you the parent. They then may grow up tackling all relationships in this manner. Be careful not to confuse your child or children with being your best friends. They only have one set of parents, and you need to retain that role by being the parents they need.

One last thing to sum up this chapter on STEP 2, consequences. Do not worry if a consequence I have given here as an example, does not work for your family dynamics. There will always be one that does work for you. This is why I give you room here in this book to jot down your own ideas that are a better fit maybe than the examples I have provided. If you think about it and plan ahead, it grows on you and becomes easier and easier every time you carry it out.

_____

_____

_____

_____

_____

_____

_____

_____

_____

_____

_____

_____

_____

_____

_____

_____

_____

CHAPTER 6

Step 3: *Apply Consistently*

STEP three is the last step in the disciplinary process, and then you're good to go! All that you have to do now is one last thing. This last step may seem impossible at times, but I am here to reassure you that it really isn't as bad as you may think initially.

This 3rd STEP is all about being consistent on follow-through with each step.

Consistency is not as hard as you may think it will be. It is really important to establish the steps as a routine, as "just the way we do things" for your family.

Having both parents using the same method of discipline will make things even more consistent, and will definitely establish a solid foundation in raising your children.

It is important to keep a positive attitude in carrying out this step of being consistent. Being positive will be most helpful in keeping you from being swayed by your child's upsetting and complaining manner when you follow through on Step 2/ Consequences, when being, **Step 3/ Consistent**.

The directions to follow with this step are plain and simple. Just don't buckle in. Keep from letting your child soften you into giving in to them.

I trust you will only have to use these steps once or twice at the most. Once a child picks up that you the parent are serious about following through and being consistent with consequences and establishing your own boundaries, they tend to test them a lot less. (Remember that it is okay for a child to speak freely and let you know appropriately how they feel about the issue at hand. This shows that they are still free to express their feelings even though they will still be held accountable for their actions).

There is one other thing that is helpful to know as a parent. When following these steps you are apt to hear your child say, "I hate you Mommy!" Not to worry, for that is to be expected. It is venting steam. Or it is a last ditch attempt to get you the parent to fold.

Don't do it! Children will experience both being frustrated with limits and having their needs met. However, they will develop an understanding that their needs are met regardless. That some wants won't be gratified. That they will have some things go their way and others not. They will learn, to their betterment, that the reality of the world is that it is not fair nor perfect, in the sense that they won't always get their own way.

Out of this they develop a balanced view of themselves as well as others.

Doing the exercises in this booklet will help you to be readily prepared and to quickly come up with on the spot, logical and natural consequences.

Remember to be consistent by following through on the consequences.

Add a description here, as to what Step 3 is all about:

_____
_____
_____
_____
_____
_____
_____
_____
_____
_____
_____
_____
_____

What message will your children get if you are inconsistent?

_____
_____
_____

What message will your children get if you are consistent?

FORMING HABITS:

I will not go into this very much for there is plenty of material out there on this subject. It is included to point out the need for these 3 STEPS to become habitual. By becoming a good habit, they no longer require much thinking beforehand to carry out. It just becomes a natural way to deal with the disciplining of your child.

It is said that it takes 21 days to break a bad habit and establish a new and better one. Erasing bad habits requires consistency over the 21 days. That means you have to stop the bad habit and not allow it to happen for the full 21 days.

Now I know that can be difficult. No need to get down on yourself. As I said earlier, keep a positive attitude throughout, and if you miss a day in the 21 days; just pick up where you left off till you achieve it. Working on this teaches your child how to succeed as well.

By building on the teaching of boundaries, your child will in turn develop good habits along with responsibility.

May I remind you to get in the habit of doing this: "PRAISE YOUR CHILD" whenever you can! There are so many ways to say it…..

i.e.: WAY TO GO! *WELL DONE! *I'm so proud of you! *BRAVO! * Fantastic * Good Job

* You're being responsible * You're special * Outstanding * Terrific * How Smart * Excellent *WOW

* Nothing can stop you now! * Super Job * Phenomenal * A+Job * Beautiful sharing * You DID IT!

* I LOVE YOU! * Keep up the good work! * You mean a lot to me! * You're a treasure * PERFECT!

* MARVELOUS * You're a WINNER! * YEAH! * You learned it right! * You did well! *

WRITE YOUR OWN COMPLIMENTS HERE:

_____
_____
_____
_____
_____
_____
_____
_____
_____
_____
_____
_____
_____
_____

CHAPTER 7:

Attitude

I am sure that you have heard over and over again that a positive attitude is everything. Well, that is true! A great attitude isn't just a good thing for your children to have. You the parents need this outlook to best handle your own lives.

You model your attitude on an ongoing basis for your children to observe and benefit from. After all, you are their primary role models on the subject of life and how to deal with it. So dealing with life in as positive way as possible is the best modeling you can provide for your children.

The discipline method is our main focus in this booklet, so we will not go into great detail on the topic of attitude specifically. Attitude of course plays an important role in helping or not helping one maintain consistency with the discipline method. It is pretty clear that the parents need to keep a positive attitude no matter how difficult it may get.

The good news that will help you keep a positive attitude is that if you plan, communicate clearly, and remain consistent you WILL be successful.

Keeping a positive attitude toward being consistent makes it easier to be consistent and ultimately succeed.

It is quite crucial to keep a positive attitude when being consistent because that is what makes the steps bearable and all worthwhile! It can be difficult to begin with, to implement planned and consistent discipline. Being positive will be most helpful in keeping you on task, and will aid in persistence and endurance.

It will keep you from being swayed by your child's upsets and complaining. You may see this aspect as too hard to put up with and endure. I assure you it will pass before you realize it and you will find it short-lived. After all, choice and your ability are always within you to resist your child's outbursts or protests.

Note, however, when speaking to your child or children as you lay down the consequences by being consistent in your follow through; you need to do so in a neutral manner. Remember as the parent you are always on display to your children. Therefore it is important to continue modeling control. Hence the neutral calm composure. It is important to be neutral in tone, and keep your facial expression neutral and your posture relaxed as you state these steps in a matter of fact way.

A child will give you a rebellious attitude, no doubt. That is to be expected. You see, it is natural for them to rebel. It is part of their learning process by which they grow, and develop the ability to speak out what is on their mind in appropriate ways. Don't let your children's rebellious attitude get to yours and ruin it.

It is your attitude that is most crucial here. You will teach and model to your child proper attitude. So their attitude will in turn grow into an appropriate form of attitude and not remain in the state that of a tantrum-filled two year old. Maintaining a positive attitude is an essential tool for children to grow up having in their arsenal to combat that world out there. The world deals out all kinds of logical and natural consequences daily. To be able to have a good attitude is crucial for how well they bear up under it all.

It is key to realize that a child's protest isn't reality. Nor is a child's protest wrong or right as to what is good. When your child is hurting or suffering pain from natural consequences, keep in mind it is not a bad thing that is going on for him or her. The positive outcome far outweighs their grief in the moment. In the long run they learn:

- From reality that life is not pain free.
- That they are not to avoid what is considered reasonable pain or exhaust themselves in trying to prevent it.
- To value life with pain by understanding its place. They learn to make "good" pain a teacher, ally and guide.

Positive thinking helps one feel good overall, and that in turn instills healthy living and parenting.

CHAPTER 8:

Being Assertive While Communicating

I have noted in previous chapters that it is essential for parents to speak with a neutral, matter–of–fact type of tone. Well, that is required in the use of the method of communication described in this chapter.

Assertive Communication is the best way to relay your expectations and or how you feel, to others in a healthy way. It is a method that transmits your expectations and feelings in a non-judgmental way. It does not point fingers or cast blame. When you explain your point of view or your feelings, you will not be saying it in an accusatory way that tends to automatically point fingers at someone(s). Assertive Communications usually prevents people from getting on the defensive. You certainly do not want defensiveness! For there is no advantage to that and it usually gets you nowhere.

Here are a couple of examples of assertive communicating:

EXAMPLE:
"I am hurt when I am spoken to in this way."

The above is healthy statement whereby one states what they do not like without pointing blame in a neutral, non-aggressive way.

EXAMPLE:
"I can't drive safely when there is so much noise in the car. I need it to be quieter before I can continue on."

This explains the reasons for having low noise in a non-emotional way, that focuses on the behavior rather than blaming the person.

Think of things you don't like, and would like to communicate to others and

try writing them down here in an assertive way:

WHAT AM I GOING TO DO WITH THIS CHILD?

CHAPTER 9:

Planning Your Activities

Remember when I spoke of not worrying if you could not come up with a logical consequence, and said that I had a solution for that to share later? Yes, there may be times when you won't have any ideas filed away in your mind to come up with. That is perfectly okay, for as I said, I do have a solution to that as well. In the meantime, just to review, we parents need to file in our memory banks a few logical consequences as laid out in STEP 2.

Then the key to using them is consistency as described in STEP 3.

When sticking to the plan by using these steps in a consistent manner we can't fail. My successful kids are proof of that. Consistency is key and that is the 3rd and primary STEP!

The thought-out ahead list of consequences prevents you the parent from taking the brunt of the deal. As I have mentioned, I prepared myself ahead of time so I did not have to endure the consequences along with my kids when I held them accountable. You will recall that one way I did this was to carry a good novel or book of short stories that I enjoyed reading. So I was ready if I did have to pop out of a performance or game or some other event because my infant or toddler was going into a fit of crying that was not the result of their usual needs not being met. In other words, they did not need to be fed or changed, etc. They were just being their toddler self with attitude. If the consequence meant me having to take my child out of the room or event until they settled down, and the deal was they could go back when they calmed down, I made sure I had something to enjoy myself with, like a favourite book or crocheting. Hence I was not suffering from their misbehaving. You might use these ideas, or even have a game or book on your cell phone to enjoy while you wait if you have to when following through and serving a consequence.

🖉 Please list below and/or set up on your phone apps. and things you would enjoy doing if you were to, have to wait, in cases where your child has to take time to settle down and stop to change their bad behaviour in order to get control of themselves:

_____
_____
_____
_____
_____
_____
_____
_____
_____
_____
_____
_____
_____
_____
_____

If you have a list then you will be prepared. That will make things a whole lot easier to handle.

CHAPTER 10:

Conclusion

There you go! 3 Easy Steps you can take and be a success at parenting. I know for I followed the steps, and it works! As I mentioned much earlier, it has been a way of parenting I came up with. It is something that I compiled from out of books, ideas and trials and errors of my own when I became a parent. Since it worked so well with my own three strong-willed children and through my coaching and teaching over the years, I presented it to parents when teaching post-graduate continuing education courses. Hence, I felt parents of today would be greatly helped by my sharing the simple 3 step discipline process.

It worked very well for my own children and those of my students, and also for my many students over the years. I was asked to handle the difficult subbing jobs, because I could keep students in control and easily discipline them. I received four nominations for "Teacher of the Year, Student Choice Awards." That was due mainly to my discipline and creative teaching that kept the students in line and doing what was assigned to them while under my supervision.

I said at the beginning of this book that I had one final secret to reveal that will set your whole mind at ease about using the 3 disciplinary steps. Here is the secret:

Consistency is not as hard as you think it will be. Once you plan and make the 3 steps a habit, which only takes a few weeks, then you can use them easily. Effective discipline means that you will use it less and less often as your children learn to self-control. They'll soon realize that there's no good reason to continue misbehaving.

Remember the following keys, and you are well on your way to extreme parenting success!

- The earlier the age you start with your children the easier it will be for all concerned.

- Plan consequences ahead

- Use a calm and normal voice and neutral facial expression to describe appropriate behavior.

- Plan things to do if you will have to wait while your kids comply.

- Remain very calm and unemotional while carrying out consequences.

KAREN MCKENZIE SMITH

IN SUMMARY

I can guarantee that you can be consistent and follow through. Just make sure you do it at least twice on an issue. For I assure you that chances are very likely you will only have to be consistent a few times to establish a consistent disciplinarian pattern. Stick in there! Once established, your child or children will see there is no point in trying to get out of the consequences.

So you see, this little secret of mine will set your mind at ease about carrying out these 3 STEPS that are truly easy to follow. The only time it will be more of a challenge is when you have to start instilling these STEPS when your children are at a much older age.

The older the child is when you start using these STEPS, of course the harder it will be. The younger your children are when you start to incorporate these STEPS, the easier it will be for you. The older they are, the harder it will be to turn the bad habit into good. But, with consistency and calmness, you will prevail!

I have said this already, but it bears repeating. By using these 3 easy steps to discipline, you are benefiting your child.

To conclude, who should bear the repercussions of naughty behaviour? You or the child? A great clue to picking out the right consequence is to pick one that is going to cost them something and NOT you. Choose something of VALUE to them personally, and know that by depriving them of a toy or treat for their misbehaviours today, you are raising a strong adult for tomorrow.

Remember when you select a consequence, the best kind are ones that involve things the child values and will not want to forego. What good is it to give them a consequence that they really do not care about? That is not a good choice of consequence for your child.

Like these examples. Don't

- Send them to their room only for them to get to play games on their computer or X-box.

Or

- Make them miss music practice or something they may not want to go to and do in the first place.

Choose consequences that will be effective and then, follow through. Remember to be consistent! Follow-through is essential for this disciplinary method to work.

That alone will help you remain determined to be consistent. For the benefits far outweigh the cons for both parents and child.

**There you go!
3 easy steps you can take and be a success at parenting. I know, for I did it as a parent, teacher and instructor and it was successful. It works!**

FINALLY,

I lift a prayer of blessing that the Lord watch over you and help you be the best disciplinarian you can be!

Remember, terrible twos and tantrums need not last forever.

The same goes for strong-willed children.

With your consistency as a parent, they will adjust to this method and become appreciative to you for setting boundaries and establishing how they should act.

They will see, learning to behave well is in their best interest!

This end is just your beginning!

*You can do it!
I pray you do, Amen!*

TA-DAH!

You've passed!

Now, reap the benefits of being an even more successful parent, for they have the most fun with their kids.

About the Author:

Karen McKenzieSmith is a published author, speaker and counsellor. She is also a parent, and an award-winning Alberta certified teacher. She has taught numerous courses on child discipline.

This booklet was published in response to the many requests she has had from parents and community experts to put her effective, simple and no nonsense approach in writing.

Karen can be reached at karencowgirl@shaw.ca

CPSIA information can be obtained
at www.ICGtesting.com
Printed in the USA
LVHW05s1616231018
594537LV00010B/467/P